MARY VIRGINIA FOX

Franklin Watts
New York/London/Toronto/Sydney/1987
A First Book

Cover photograph courtesy of Shostal

Photographs courtesy of:
Ohio Department of Natural Resources: pp. 10
(Richard Moseley), 12, 13, 16 (Herb Hott), 50,
65 (bottom); Ohio Historical Society: pp 19,
21, 22, 28, 30, 34, 37, 41, 47; NCR Corp.:
p. 44; Convention & Visitors Bureau of Greater
Cleveland: p. 54 (top-Mark C. Schwartz);
Mort Tucker Photography, Inc.: p. 54 (bottom);
Greater Cincinnati Convention & Visitors
Bureau: pp. 56, 58; Firestone Tire & Rubber
Company: p. 60 (top); Libbey Glass: p. 60
(bottom); Youngstown/Warren Business Journal:
p. 63; Ohio Department of Development: pp. 64,
65 (top-David Lucas); NASA: p. 66.

Library of Congress Cataloging-in-Publication Data

Fox, Mary Virginia.
Ohio.

(A First book)
Bibliography: p.
Includes index.
Summary: Discusses the history, politics, industry,
natural resources, economy, people, and large cities
of Ohio.
1. Ohio—Juvenile literature. [1. Ohio] I. Title.
F491.3.F69 1987   977.1   87-6179
ISBN 0-531-10392-7

CONTENTS

Chapter One
The Land
7

Chapter Two
Settling In
15

Chapter Three
Transportation
24

Chapter Four
Culture Moves West
32

Chapter Five
Ohio and the Civil War
36

Chapter Six
Industry and Labor
39

Chapter Seven
Politics
46

Chapter Eight
Keeping the Water Clean
49

Chapter Nine
Cities and People
53

For Further Reading
68

Index
69

OHIO

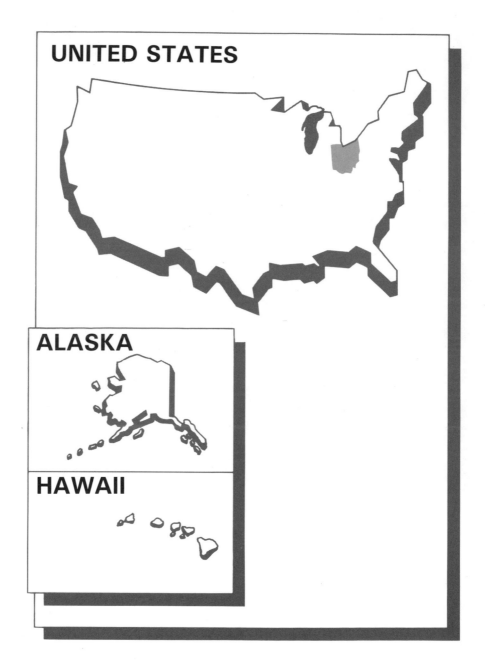

UNITED STATES

ALASKA

HAWAII

THE LAND

When you fly over the state of Ohio during the lush growing season of summer, you look down upon a vast patchwork of fields spiked with great cities and industrial belts. The state is laced together with ribbons of paved highways and waterways.

The Ohio River, one of the great rivers of North America, cuts a sweeping boundary for more than 450 miles (724 km) along Ohio's southern and southeastern borders.

To the north, the state of Ohio stretches for 312 miles (502.11 km) along the shores of Lake Erie, from Conneaut in the east to Toledo in the west, giving access to ocean trade by ship through the St. Lawrence Seaway.

Ohio has more than 44,000 miles (70,400 km) of rivers and streams that flow either south into the Ohio River or north into Lake Erie, a fact that greatly helped open the land for settlement. From outer space, Ohio would seem almost square, reaching 225 miles (363.10 km) from east to west and 210 miles (337.96 km) from north to south.

The general surface of the state is a rolling plain, with rounded hills and valleys in the west and more rugged, steeper terrain in the east.

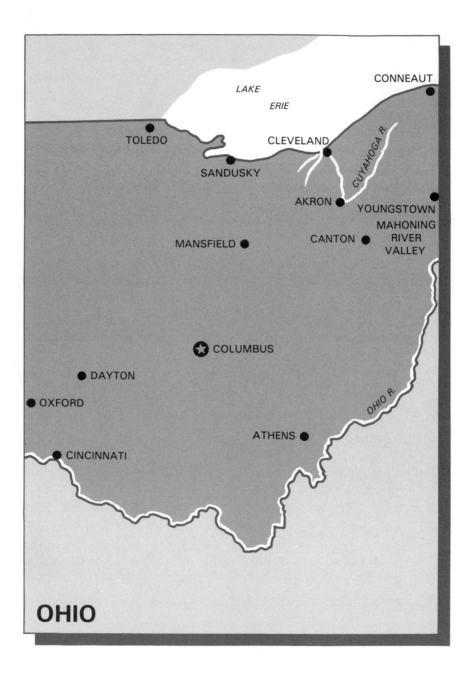

LAKE ERIE

CONNEAUT

TOLEDO

CLEVELAND

CUYAHOGA R.

SANDUSKY

AKRON

YOUNGSTOWN

MANSFIELD

CANTON

MAHONING RIVER VALLEY

★ COLUMBUS

DAYTON

OXFORD

OHIO R.

ATHENS

CINCINNATI

OHIO

Ohio is abundantly rich in mineral resources. It owes this fertile bed of soil and subsurface wealth to its past history.

Millions of years ago, water covered everything. Gradually the land tilted upward. The water drained off, and luxuriant growth appeared in the swamps. But other changes were about to take place. Bitter cold gripped the northern part of the hemisphere. A huge mantle of ice, as much as a mile (almost 2 km) thick, pressed down upon the land. The ice came and went six times. It scraped the land flat.

During the longest of the glacial ages, the great ice sheet formed a colossal dam, a mile (1.61 km) high and fifty miles (80.47 km) long. This created an inland sea that geologists call "Lake Ohio." This ancient lake was 400 miles (643.74 km) long and 200 miles (321.87 km) across and drowned the future site of Pittsburgh under 300 feet (91.44 m) of water.

When the ice finally disappeared, a thick, rich layer of soil was spread over the inland regions of what is now known as the state of Ohio. Underground lay beds of clay, sand, salt, coal, gas, oil, iron ore, and limestone, materials for which modern people have found many uses. Only in the southeastern part of the territory, where the ice had not reached, are there deep, jagged valleys and rocky land.

When the climate warmed to what we now think of as normal, the seeds that were strewn over the bare dirt caught hold, and a dense forest grew. Small animals darted between the giant trees, and in the clearings, where there was forage, deer abounded. Bears made their dens in protected places.

Finally humans followed animals into the rich hunting land. From about 800 B.C. to A.D. 1500 the Adena and Hopewell cultures, collectively called the Moundbuilders, flourished. They grew crops, traded, made fine carved pipes and ornaments, and left impressive burial grounds and mounds scattered throughout the state. It was not until white people came that written history left a record of the Ohio Valley.

Glacial movements had helped create the state's four main

A portion of the Little Miami River.
This picturesque river—105 miles in length—
flows through deep gorges, steep and wooded hills,
pleasant farmlands, and small towns.

land areas. The Great Lakes Plains of northern Ohio spread from the shore of Lake Erie south, a distance that varies from 10 miles (16.09 km) in the east to more than 50 miles (80.47 km) in the Maumee Valley to the west. A wide variety of crops grows in this fertile strip of land. Grape vineyards and fruit orchards line the shores of Lake Erie. The moderating temperature of the lake prevents early budding in the spring, which could be harmed by fluctuating freezing temperatures.

The region is one of the busiest manufacturing, shipping, and trading areas in the United States. It includes many lake ports and industrial cities, Cleveland being one of the largest in the state.

The Till Plains take over the western part of the state. They are ranked as one of the most fertile farming areas in the country, part of the great midwestern corn belt. Farmers also produce a great deal of grain and livestock. The area has several large industrial cities where a variety of products is manufactured. Both the highest point in the state, Campbell Hill, which rises to 1,550 feet (472 m), and the lowest point in Hamilton County, 433 feet (132 m), are found in this region.

The Appalachian Plateau includes almost all of the eastern half of the state. This high land extends eastward into Pennsylvania and West Virginia. It has some of the most beautiful scenery in Ohio, with deep valleys, waterfalls, and the state's largest forests. It also has rich mineral deposits—clay, coal, natural gas, oil, salt, limestone, and gypsum.

The Bluegrass Region is a small triangle of land in southern Ohio, an extension of the Bluegrass Region of Kentucky. There are gently rolling hills, but here the soil layer is thin and not as rich as the plains to the north.

Ohio's climate is controlled by cold dry fronts from Canada and warm moist fronts from the Gulf of Mexico. When the fronts meet, predictably rain results, much needed for farm production. Ohio's precipitation totals 38 inches (97 cm). The normal average temperature in the state ranges from 56 degrees Fahrenheit (13.3 c)

Ohio is part of the great midwestern corn belt.

*These before (left) and after photographs show how
soil conservation efforts are working in the state.
The strip-mined area was restored to productive use.*

at Portsmouth in the south to 47 degrees Fahrenheit (8.33 c) at Dorset in the northeast.

The soil and climate are suited to a variety of crops. Corn occupies less than one-third of the crop land, but usually accounts for about 60 percent of the total crop value. Soybeans and hay rank high, and sugar beets are grown in the northwestern part of the state.

Raising dairy and beef cattle, hogs, and poultry are popular farming occupations. The production of milk, butter, and cheese, especially Liederkranz, has become increasingly important to Ohio's economy.

Because Ohio is centrally located, its farmers are close to the nation's biggest markets. Ohio ranks seventh among the states in the value of its crops.

Soil conservation is particularly emphasized in the gully-ridden hills of the southeast. Trees are now being planted to replace those that have been stripped from the land.

Ohio stands sixth among the nation's states in population, though it is only thirty-fifth in area. Its industrial strength and commercial importance to the entire country are far more significant than its size. Nearly four-fifths of the leading industries in the nation are found in Ohio. Its industries produce iron and steel, rubber products, all types of machine tools and heavy equipment, and glass and pottery.

Much has happened since the first white people came to explore the land we know as Ohio.

SETTLING IN

The Indians first encountered by the white people were relatively recent immigrants to the area. Three hundred years ago, five tribes, numbering not more than about fifteen thousand people, made this vast tract their home. They were the Shawnee, Wyandot, Miami, Ottawa, and Delaware. They were mainly hunters. They knew how to plant corn, pumpkin, and beans, but most of the land was forest. It was easier to hunt meat than to fell trees and farm the land with crude stone axes.

The first white people came looking for a route to China. Rene-Robert Cavalier, Sieur de la Salle, heard the Indians talk about a great river known as the O-hy-o which flowed to the west. He was excited. This might be the passage he had been searching for. In 1699 La Salle set out to explore the waterway. The Indian word "O-hy-o" meant "something great."

La Salle was not to be disappointed. The Ohio is a river that does not start as a trickle of water in some hidden forest. The Monongahela and the Allegheny rivers, where Pittsburgh now stands, give birth to the Ohio in a massive flow that carves a valley to the west. La Salle came to explore, not to settle. It was the French traders who first came to know the Ohio Valley and to claim the

land. They learned how to survive in the wilderness by studying the Indian ways. They made their fires out of white oak bark that sent up little smoke, to keep their presence a secret. They guided themselves by the moss on tree trunks and the stars overhead.

The French spoke the Indian tongues and could make their meaning clear using sign language. The Indians made them their brothers and, in return, the French painted their faces and smoked a peace pipe. These early adventurers lived a border life between two worlds, the hearth fires of their people and the council fires of the Indians.

In contrast, the early English who ventured on the wilderness trails rarely lived Indian-style. They thought of the red people as savages. But they would not be denied this plentiful land at their back door. Directly west of the Alleghenies, Ohio naturally caught the first waves of westward expansion from the colonists who had established homes on the eastern seaboard.

By the middle of the eighteenth century, as many as three hundred English traders were crossing the highlands each year and fanning out from the waters of the Ohio and the great lake of Erie. The most important trade routes followed the land bridges, or portages, that linked the north-south waterways: the Maumee and Miami rivers, the Sandusky and Scioto rivers, and the Cuyahoga, Tuscarawas, and Muskingum rivers were the highways through the forests.

There was an abundance of game for food and, more important, for furs to be traded for wealth. There were beaver, fox, and deer

To walk through Lake Katharine State Nature Preserve is to walk back in time to the wilderness of Ohio. One can see sandstone bluffs and rock shelters, deep ravines laced with remnant glacial plants, and a clear-water lake.
—17

for anyone willing to suffer a trader's hardships. A buckskin sold for a dollar in the eastern market. Even today, a dollar is still known as a buck.

To protect their trading posts, military forts were built by both the French and English. Too late, the Indians realized the white people's appetite for land was never satisfied. And they watched as the whites fought among themselves and tried to bribe the Indians to be on their side.

The French and Indian War eliminated the French. In 1763 they ceded their possessions east of the Mississippi to the British.

It was not until the British lost the War of Independence with the colonists that George III turned over all claim to this land to the new United States.

The Territorial Congress enacted the Land Ordinance of 1785, which called for the purchase of land from the Indian inhabitants and for its survey and sale to frontier settlers. The Northwest Territory was established in July 1787 as "the territory northwest of the River Ohio." It consisted of the region west of the state of Pennsylvania between the Ohio and Mississippi rivers. Prescribed laws were set up to provide a system of government for the entire region.

In 1794 the backbone of all Indian resistance was broken at the Battle of Fallen Timbers. With peace, there was time for men to dream of the fertile Ohio Valley to the west as a place to settle, not just as a place to trap and trade. Many hesitated to expose their families to the dangers of wilderness living, but groups began banding together to form communities for added protection and security.

Whole villages sometimes pulled up stakes and moved west. Those from Norwalk, Connecticut, founded Norwalk, Ohio, and Granville, Massachusetts, gave birth to Granville, Ohio.

The northeastern corner of Ohio, known as the Western Reserve because it was land that had been reserved for war veterans, had originally been owned by the state of Connecticut. Towns sprang up along the shoreline of Erie, with familiar patterns from the East: town squares, white churches, and orderly governments.

The Ohio Company recruited twenty men, four women, and two

*Heading west for Ohio (note the word "Ohio"
on the wagon side) from Massachusetts*

boys to mark out a town at the mouth of the Little Miami, the site of Cincinnati. Except for military outposts, this was the most westerly settlement on the Ohio.

Life on the frontier naturally fostered democratic ideals. These were hardy, independent, God-fearing backwoods farmers who shunned the aristocratic commercial atmosphere of the Atlantic seaboard. There was obvious equality of wealth and equality of hardships endured. Independence was cherished, yet a certain co-operative dependence was required for survival.

The first families to come to Ohio after it was opened for settlement were those from the eastern seaboard. They were looking for rich farmland. The best had already been taken in the original colonies. They had only to cross one mountain range, and within a week or two, they could choose where they would settle.

New Englanders were especially numerous in the Western Reserve of the northeast, while people from Virginia and Kentucky came into the southern part of the state. Most of these early settlers were of English descent, but in the east and south there were many of Scotch-Irish or German stock, the latter called Pennsylvania Dutch. After 1830 large numbers of immigrants came directly from Ireland and Germany.

During the 1830s, many in Ireland were suffering real hardships because of crop failures. Hunger was what sent them searching for new homes. It was mainly the Irish who helped dig the canals, lay the track for rail lines, and grade the trails for roads. They were a hard-working and thrifty people. They settled largely in the cities, while the Germans who came in great numbers at this time were looking for farms. Later, some became wealthy merchants, but their beginnings were on the land.

The original land law of 1787 was passed to raise federal funds. Two dollars an acre seems like a give-away price now, but the original restriction set a minimum purchase of 640 acres. Very few frontier farmers had cash on hand to invest in a homestead, but eastern speculators did. People with money hired others to stake their claims by blazing four-corner "witness trees." Sometimes the

The first house built in Cincinnati

The Perry Memorial at Put-in-Bay,
scene of the 1812 naval battle with
the British during the War of 1812

land was cleared and planted; more often it was left as an item on a recorded deed.

Knowledgeable farmers could judge soil even in dense woods. White oak, walnut, hickory, beech, and sugar maple signified good ground, but "never blaze your corners on locust, swamp oak, or sycamore" was the warning.

In 1803 Ohio became the seventeenth state in the Union, the first to be carved from the Northwest Territory. The legislature first met in the old territorial capital of Chillicothe. When it was felt that a more central location was required, the official capital was moved to Zanesville in 1810, where it remained until 1812.

However, four merchants from Franklin County had even grander ideas for a state capital. They were sure to make a profit by such a move, but no one seemed to care when the generous offer of ten acres for a statehouse and ten acres for a penitentiary were granted to the new city's charter. Also, fifty thousand dollars was pledged as a donation for the erection of these buildings. As an added bonus, half an acre was given as a public graveyard.

Thus Columbus was born. The first town lots on High and Broad streets were sold for from two hundred to five hundred dollars, a stiff price for land no one had wanted the year before.

Ohio was prospering. Most of the warring Indians had been pushed west. The rivers continued to handle traffic. Suddenly, this peaceful progress was brought to a halt by the War of 1812.

The British still had their eye on a slice of America. Americans had their hopes on expansion into Canada. The control of Lake Erie was the focal point of Ohio's role in the war. Oliver Hazard Perry's rout of the British fleet at Put-in-Bay, soon followed by General William Harrison's victory on the Canadian Thames, definitely secured the West for the United States. Tecumseh's death in the Battle of the Thames ended the Indian support of the British and dealt a further blow to their dwindling resistance.

New treaties were signed, and the British gave up all claims to the land south of the Great Lakes. Again Ohio was ready for development, and this time with no enemies to fight.

TRANSPORTATION

Between 1800 and 1820 the population of Ohio multiplied seven times. Between 1820 and 1845 the population doubled, then doubled again. By 1850 Ohio was the third most populous state in the nation, an amazing display of growth considering that a few years before, the land had been wilderness.

As more and more of the virgin forest was cut down for towns and farms, there was a great need for improved transportation. Farmers could produce bumper crops, but there was no way to get their produce to market. One solution was to reduce bulky items into produce more easily transported. Grain was ground into flour or distilled into whiskey. Corn was fed to hogs. Almost every Ohio community had at least one distillery, one gristmill, and a slaughterhouse. Because of these three products for market, Cincinnati became the first industrial metropolis of the West.

In 1796 Ebenezer Zane had been authorized by Congress to build a road from the Ohio River opposite Wheeling, West Virginia, to the Ohio River opposite Maysville, Kentucky, cutting across the southeastern corner of Ohio. It was unpaved and rutted with heavy traffic. Zane's Trace, as it was called, was the first highway west, the only road in the entire Northwest Territory.

In the spring it turned into a quagmire of mud, and in certain sections was completely impassable for wagon trains. Improvements were started in 1811 with funds from the federal treasury. In the eastern part of the state, the trail followed the original course of Zane's Trace, but it branched out to cut across the middle of the state. The new road was cleared and graded and surfaced with crushed stone.

The National Road was blocked with tollgates every twenty miles (32.19 km) with a tollman's cottage close by. The revenue collected went to maintenance and repair. The road was not completed until 1840, but it opened a whole new corridor into the interior. Great lumbering Conestoga wagons hauled by six-horse teams carried freight back and forth across the state.

These wagoners spoke a language of their own. They were the forerunners of the cross-country truckers of today. They dressed alike in blue denim trousers and blue flannel hunting shirts trimmed in red. They congregated at stage stops along the way to bunk for the night. These stops were the beginnings of many a village turned town and city in later years.

Stagecoaches for passenger travel were faster, but not necessarily more comfortable. It was a rough ride even with improvements. Today you can travel the same route on a smooth pavement by following U.S. Highway 40.

By far the most popular means of transportation in the early days was still aboard any craft that would float down the water highways of the state and across the great lake of Erie. A few near-ocean-size sailing schooners made their way the length of Lake Erie, dropping off new settlers at harbors whose docks jutted from recently cleared forests. Cleveland and Toledo were only nicks in the wilderness, but soon grew to be important ports.

It was on the Ohio River that boats varied from the simplest rafts to keel boats capable of hauling considerable tonnage. It wasn't unusual to see a floating barnyard in passing. Planks hastily lashed together frequently were the turf for the family cow, horse, pigs, and chickens. These flat-bottomed square boxes were called broad-

—25

horns because of twin sweeps, or long-handled oars, near the square bow that kept the craft in the river channel. When a landing was made, the raft was broken up into pieces and salvaged for the first home in the wilderness.

The keel boats were built to last. Some were as large as 60 feet (18.29 m) in length with a 10- or 12-foot (3.05- or 3.66-m) beam. They had a shaped stern and were fitted with a mast and sail. However, when the channel narrowed and there was no room for maneuvering, poles and oars were used for the upstream trips.

By the 1820s steamboats added a grander form of transportation. They never quite equaled the Mississippi fleet, but they were designed to skim over the shallows when the water line was low. The river was always changing. One summer the mid-channel depth at Cincinnati measured twenty-three inches (58.42 cm). Two years later the Ohio rose sixty feet (18.29 m). It wasn't until much later that the river was tamed with locks and dams.

Waterways leading into the interior of the state were badly needed. The four canoe passages between Lake Erie and the Ohio were still in use, but each demanded laborious overland portages. Even before the Revolutionary War, visionaries had suggested connecting the north-south tributaries with hand-dug ditches. At the time it seemed a rather foolish venture through wilderness territory, but the land was now filling with settlers.

In 1823, while the Erie Canal connecting the Hudson River to Lake Erie was nearing completion, Ohio Governor Jeremiah Morrow sent to New York for engineer James Geddess. Geddess had helped survey the Erie Canal in New York State.

Geddess spent several months studying the old Indian-trapper routes and came up with two alternate suggestions. Proving that the new state had great plans for the future, funds were pledged for the building of both canals.

On July 4, 1825, the first shovelful of earth was turned for the Ohio Canal at Newark, Ohio. Three weeks later at Middletown, Ohio, the Miami-Erie Canal was started.

For several years, the canal project gave employment to a steady stream of immigrants from across the Atlantic. The Irish made up the first wave of muscle workers. They earned thirty cents a day and were housed and fed. Next came the Norwegians and the Welsh.

One section of the canal was dug by people who sang hymns and preached the strict gospel of the Zoarites. They earned enough cash to buy twelve thousand acres for their religious community, with enough money left over to set up a profitable tannery, brickyard, and ore furnace.

By the late 1830s, more than a thousand miles (1,609.35 km) of canal were under construction. When money was in short supply, convicts were used to keep the work going. A time schedule was set for completion.

Locks had to be engineered to step the barges up and down the slight rise in the middle of the state. It was here the first cabins that were to be the beginnings of towns were built. The city of Akron was situated at the highest point of the Ohio-Erie Canal—hence its name, which is a Greek word meaning high point. Eventually, a branch canal connected this waterway directly with Pittsburgh, which made Akron the leading inland port of the West.

The canals made the state a unified region. Farmers' products that had never had a market past the next settlement now were loaded onto barges and shipped east. And in the opposite direction, salted venison reached New Orleans by way of the river-canal route. Produce multiplied in value. Canal boats hauled out lumber and returned with steam engines for gristmills.

Mills, brick ovens, and iron foundries were built along the waterways. Another product was salt. Throughout the southeastern part of the state were salt licks that animals and Indians had used for centuries. Water from the salt springs was pumped to the surface, evaporated, and shipped in blocks to cities elsewhere. There were mines, too, where the salt was dug out of the ground in chunks almost as hard as stone.

—27

The Ohio-Erie Canal

In the early days, most of the wealth of the state was measured in farm products. Long before Kansas was planted with wheat, Ohio was the grain center of the country. Warehouses sprang up, and mile-long caravans of wagons waited during threshing season to dump their loads in freight barges.

Passenger packet boats were popular. They were narrow, to fit snugly through the locks, but some of the more luxurious ones carried as many as seventy-five passengers. It was an eighty-hour trip across the state from north to south. Bunks were partitioned into men's and women's sections.

The barges were powered by horses plodding along the tow paths. As many as three horses were needed to pull the heavier loads, and usually a spare animal was tethered on the stern deck as a relief replacement. The coming of low bridges was signaled with a blast of the boat's horn so that passengers sunning themselves on the top deck could duck for safety.

The canals were barely completed when their usefulness was gone. In 1835 the first railroad track in Ohio was laid over a distance of thirty-three miles (53.11 km) from Toledo to Adrian in Michigan Territory. Its first cars were drawn by horsepower on oak rails, but soon the wooden rails were capped with strips of strap iron, and in 1837 a steam engine was put into operation.

All such locomotives were built in the East. It was impossible to freight even the smaller models of a century ago by wagon to their destination. The engines had to come by boat until rail lines were expanded, and every mile of rail traffic helped put an end to the barge traffic on the canals.

Old Number 80 came from Philadelphia by way of the Hudson River and the Erie Canal to Lake Erie and finally by a sailing schooner to the port of Toledo. It attained such an awesome speed of twenty miles (32.19 km) an hour that an Ohio law gave city councils the right to regulate the speed of trains with a maximum of four miles (6.44 km) an hour when passing close to house or farm.

Twenty-four railroads were chartered in Ohio before 1840. Level terrain eased engineering problems. Now every rural community

—29

*The arrival of the railroad in Ohio
resulted in diminished canal and river traffic.*

wanted to catch hold of a spur line that would put them on a through route to market. Soon Ohio was the leading railroad state in the country.

Sandusky eyed the success of the Toledo line with jealousy. Toledo already had a canal leading inland. Surveyors from Sandusky immediately lined up their sights on a rail line to Bellevue, a distance of sixteen miles (25.75 km). The first run was made in 1839 with crowds cheering at every crossroad. The trip took forty minutes, but plans were under way to extend the line to Springfield. It was to be called the Mad River and Lake Erie line.

In the beginning, the bold dreamers planned the lines only as connecting links with already existing water routes. However, a decade later, when the rail lines were pushed parallel to the lake shore and the rivers, the practical merits of long-distance freighting was proved.

Canal and river traffic diminished, and so did the grandeur of the earliest ports that had been the hub of all trade with the West. Cincinnati had always held a commanding position on the Ohio River. It was a trading and manufacturing center. Cincinnati also had some of the most lavish homes in the West, not to mention an opera house and the stately Burnet House, "probably the best hotel in its interior and domestic arrangements of any in the world."

Cincinnati gradually was overshadowed by other cities that had been only ugly huddles of huts a generation before. Cleveland, Detroit, and Chicago came into their own with the advent of the railroad.

CULTURE
MOVES WEST

During the first half of the nineteenth century, Ohio remained predominantly an agricultural state. Farms were usually no more than a hundred acres, as large an area as one family could clear and tend without machinery. Farmers were used to working alone. They learned to be self-sufficient. Only at harvest time did neighbors come together to help each other. In winter, when weather permitted, there might be quilting bees and grain-threshing gatherings, but in the rural areas, social affairs were family affairs.

As for other cultural activities, art museums, musical groups, and formal theater were only provided in the cities, Cincinnati being particularly proud of what it offered. Columbus and the cities along Lake Erie were still too close to their wilderness beginnings.

Itinerant portrait painters sometimes called on farm families to sell their talents, and occasionally a lecturer might advertise a coming appearance in the towns growing up along the water and land routes. Theater groups might give a one-night performance under a tent, but it was a rare treat.

Church-going depended on where one lived. Traveling preachers made their rounds on regular circuits, but Bible-reading and schooling for the young were more often home activities.

Those people who had been used to more formal opportunities for education in the East were anxious to have these advantages for their children. Learning the elements of reading and writing could take place at home, but if the new state was to have doctors, lawyers, and teachers, colleges and universities would have to be provided to train them.

Education in pioneer Ohio was private and local in character until 1825, when a statewide school tax was levied for support of private education. It wasn't until the 1850s that high schools developed, largely displacing the private academies that had provided the only available secondary education. Colleges were established first.

Ohio University was founded in 1804. It was the first university in the Northwest Territory. Oberlin College was established in 1833 by a Presbyterian preacher and an Indian missionary. What made this institution so remarkable was that it was the first coeducational college in the world. Shortly after opening, it admitted black people at a time when slavery was still condoned by a majority of bordering states.

At Miami University in Oxford, Ohio, a young professor by the name of William Holmes McGuffey spent his free time writing a series of textbooks for beginning readers. Before this time, the famous *New England Primer,* with texts directly related to the Bible, was the standard reader. It began, "A is for Adam," followed by a somber verse, "In Adam's fall / We sinned all." The rest of the rhymes were just as grim.

McGuffey wrote about everyday life, leaving the gloomy preaching for Sunday's sermons. In McGuffey's *Primer*, "A" stands for ax, a familiar tool on the frontier. Poems spoke of the beauty of nature. In the readers for older children, the theme constantly stressed was that there was opportunity for all. With a bit of hard work the future would be a bright one.

McGuffey obviously fulfilled a need in this new land. McGuffey readers were printed by the thousands and tucked away in covered wagons heading even further into the new West. McGuffey's influence was felt by generation after generation of eager young readers.

By 1860 the publishers were printing two million copies a year. McGuffey readers were standard school texts in thirty-seven states. Later in the century, they were translated into Spanish and taken with American teachers into the countries of Puerto Rico and the Philippines.

Another Ohio author, Harriet Beecher Stowe, who wrote the book *Uncle Tom's Cabin,* had a tremendous influence on the parents of these readers. Her novel described the brutal treatment of slaves. She pictured poor Eliza fleeing with her child across the ice-clogged Ohio River, and told of the death of Tom, a patient, submissive slave sold to a villainous man. To be sure, not all slaveholders were so evil, but Stowe fanned the flames of hatred for such a system.

In 1862 when Mrs. Stowe was first invited to the White House to meet President Lincoln, the president greeted her with only a hint of jest when he said, "So this is the little woman who wrote the book that made this big war."

She was not the only person from Ohio who had a great influence on the outcome of the Civil War.

Harriet Beecher Stowe, an Ohio writer famous for her novel Uncle Tom's Cabin

OHIO AND THE CIVIL WAR

Before the first shot was fired in the Civil War, Ohio was a state with a clash of feelings. The southern counties had cultural, economic, and sometimes family ties with Kentucky and the slave South. The northern counties, with their New England traditions, were strongly antislavery. The National Road through Zanesville and Columbus was the state's unofficial Mason-Dixon line. Yet along the river, within sight of the Kentucky hills, there were abolitionists who actively fought in the war to free the slaves.

Among the earliest and most consistent opponents of slavery were the Quakers. Persecuted themselves by the Puritans when they attempted to settle in New England in the seventeenth century, they had moved south to the states of Virginia and the Carolinas. But over the years, they had become so disenchanted with the practice of slave-tended plantations that many had sold their land and moved to Ohio's Miami River Valley.

It was these gentle activists who organized the Underground Railroad that would eventually funnel some seventy-five thousand slaves to freedom. From three crossing points on the Ohio River, three main lines converged at a "grand central station," the home of Levi and "Aunt Katie" Coffin in Fountain City, a Quaker village.

Ulysses S. Grant

When war was declared in the spring of 1861, President Lincoln called for seventy-five thousand volunteers, of which Ohio's quota was thirteen thousand. In response, thirty thousand streamed into the state capital of Columbus. There were monumental problems. Where could the soldiers be quartered? How were they to be fed? The people of the city opened their doors to help, although there seemed to be no military leader to take charge.

The Ohio troops may have started without leadership, but as the war progressed, the state could boast of some of the best-known generals of the Union army.

Ulysses S. Grant was born in Brown County near Point Pleasant. He never lost the look of a country man even when in the White House. He was "stumpy, slouchy, and stocky," but he had a relentless will and a flair for command.

Philip H. Sheridan, of Irish immigrant parents, grew up in Perry County where the National Road crossed the state. Commanding the Army of the Shenandoah, he proved an inspired leader, cheering his troops on even when the going was the most desperate.

William T. Sherman, hated in the South, was a hero in the North. He broke all the rules of warfare by leading his troops into enemy territory, often far from his reserves, thereby putting his troops in constant jeopardy. He had a quick mind and a quick temper, but the record of his victories helped the North win the war.

These three generals, as well as other leaders from Ohio—Edwin M. Stanton, Salmon P. Chase, James A. Garfield, and Rutherford B. Hayes—were all honored during the World's Fair in Chicago in 1893, when their bronze statues were unveiled in a court of honor. The people of Ohio had proved to be leaders of the nation.

6

INDUSTRY
AND
LABOR

The Civil War may have cut off Cincinnati's rich trade with the South, but it also fostered the city's industries. Shipyards launched new steamships. Factories poured out shoes, uniforms, tents, and saddles. Packing plants supplied endless barrels of beef, pork, and lard for the army. Brass and iron foundries were converted to manufacturing cannon. Old muskets were modernized on a full-scale production line at the Eagle Iron Works. And this was just one of Ohio's cities that mobilized for war. All across the state, small manufacturing centers grew into bigger complexes.

The first farm machinery manufactured on a large scale came from Ohio factories during the war. With men off to war, women and children were the first to use these labor-saving devices. Farms would have largely been untended otherwise.

When peace returned, factories continued to be built, and the state's industrial capabilities began to break records. Ohio was essentially rural in the first half of the 1800s, but commercial development flourished in the second half of the century.

The Ohio River served the state's southern cities, while Lake Erie helped the North grow. There were people who knew how to take advantage of the resources available. Alec Chance started as a commercial fisherman on the big lake at the port of Sandusky. He built an icehouse and stored his fish until they could be shipped to bigger markets. His company was advertised as the greatest fish market in the world. Then he took his profits and invested in still other enterprises. Sandusky claimed to have the biggest wagon-wheel works and the biggest oar factory in the country.

Another man who earned his first fortune in Ohio was Henry Flagler. He sold grain in Cleveland through a young commission merchant by the name of John D. Rockefeller. Rockefeller had several business interests himself, the most speculative being a refinery he had built to extract kerosine from crude oil.

In 1859 a well had been drilled in Titusville, Pennsylvania, that produced petroleum. When the first oil was pumped from the ground, local farmers fired up their own household stills to refine the product. With the instant demand and the immense quantity available, Rockefeller was one of the first to recognize profit in the wholesale end of the industry. He organized the Standard Oil Company and soon had established a monopoly of the refining business by cornering the supply of oil.

By the age of twenty-eight, Rockefeller had his own pipelines and tank cars bringing crude oil to his refineries in Cleveland. He also owned the ships that carried the kerosine to eastern ports and from there to Europe. He bragged that every day twenty acres of oak forest were consumed to produce the daily need of ten thousand barrels in which the oil was shipped around the world.

Around Findlay, Ohio, another underground treasure was tapped. One lucky well digger struck gas instead of water. He quickly capped the line and piped it to his own hearth to use for heat and cooking. The only problem was that he had more than he needed. Some enterprising Findlay residents formed a company to finance a deeper well. It erupted with a plume of fire one hundred feet (30.48 m) high that could be seen for forty miles (64.37 km).

An early refinery

When it was brought under control, it was realized that the people had a bonanza. Profit from the modest sum of drilling was enormous. Some of the preachers in the area predicted that the fires of hell had been tapped and the end of the world was near. It didn't seem to scare many individuals.

The discovery of this new economical fuel made Ohio the center for the manufacture of glass and clay products.

Cleveland's iron and steel industry grew, thanks to its geographic location. Vast coal beds lay in Ohio's Hocking Valley. Limestone quarries lined the shores of Lake Huron, and huge deposits of iron ore had been discovered on the upper peninsula shores of Lake Superior. Passage through the Great Lakes made it easy to transport bulk cargoes to the ports of Lake Erie.

The coal industry has always brought wealth to the state. Ships and engines that had used wood to fire their boilers now switched to the more efficient fuel, coal. Machines were invented to pick up railroad cars bodily to dump their loads into waiting hoppers and put the empty cars back on rails again for the trip back to the mines.

Ohio can brag of a whole list of inventors and their marvelous new ideas. Some were as seemingly insignificant as John Leon Bennett's wire fly swatter or a Columbus man's locomotive cowcatcher that was built to ease wandering livestock off the tracks. Dr. Edwin Beeman's flavored chewing gum was another Ohio first, and a Reynoldsburg seed merchant developed the first edible tomato. Henry Timkin's roller bearings and Armco's revolutionary rolling mill helped develop industry.

In 1870 Benjamin Franklin Goodrich watched a neighbor's house burn to the ground because a canvas fire hose burst. Goodrich figured there had to be something better—rubber, for instance. Rubber had long been considered a useless product. An English chemist had found it would rub out pencil marks—hence the name rubber —but that was all it was good for, everybody thought.

About the same time that Goodrich started the Anchor Fire Hose Company in Akron, young Harvey Firestone thought of making rubber rims for buggy wheels. A much more complicated process was developed by the Seiberling Brothers, who produced tires filled with air. They named their company after a Mister Charles Goodyear, who had earlier patented a process for vulcanizing rubber. He died penniless, but his name lived on. As the motor industry developed, so did their business. In ten years, Akron's population increased threefold.

One man from Dayton made money from money itself. John Ritty invented a mechanical money drawer that recorded figures like an adding machine and rang a bell whenever the drawer was opened. It started out as an amusing toy, but John Patterson could see a future for the gadget. He bought the idea from Ritty for $6,500 and began manufacturing the new cash registers on an assembly line. This was the beginning of the NCR Corporation.

One of Patterson's salesmen, Thomas J. Watson, went on to found the International Business Machines Corporation, a company that turned ordinary cash registers into a legacy of computer products.

One of the most famous inventors of all time, Thomas Alva Edison, developed his scientific curiosity as a small boy in the Ohio town of Milan. What would the world have done without his electric light, phonograph recording device, and dozens of other technical discoveries?

Orville and Wilbur Wright made test flights in their first power-driven airplane from a field near Dayton.

The aluminum refining process was discovered by Charles M. Hall. New ideas were continually being turned into products, and more and more factories were being built. As the state changed from a farming community to one of factories and heavy industry, many people saw dangers ahead.

With so much wealth funneling into the pockets of a few millionaires who had early seized control of industry, the United States Congress realized that laws were needed to regulate big business. John Sherman, brother of the Civil War general, proposed an an-

titrust law that was enacted in 1890. This law was meant to keep any one company from having exclusive control of an industry.

The first company found guilty was Rockefeller's Standard Oil. Rockefeller simply sold some of his interests to an independent company then called Ohio Oil and later Marathon, but he continued to earn a fortune.

Ohio was a state that nurtured labor unions along with industrial development. These were organizations of workers who had banded together to fight for better working conditions and pay from the powerful companies that employed them.

Some of the bitterest labor disputes were in the coal industry. Eighteen eighty-four was not a good year. Coal had been stockpiled, wages cut, and several thousand miners were out of work. The miners went on strike for better working conditions, but the owners brought in outsiders to carry on the diggings.

The strikers attacked by dumping barrels of oil onto coal cars and then sending them blazing into the tunnels. This underground fire has been smoldering ever since, destroying millions of dollars of valuable coal. Governor George Hoadley ordered out the state militia and there was violence on both sides. The strike was finally settled, but the miners felt a stronger bargaining organization was needed in the future.

In 1885 the Ohio Federation of Labor was formed. The next year a convention of labor leaders from other states was held in Columbus. The American Federation of Labor was born with Samuel Gompers at its head. Two years later, in Columbus, the United Mine Workers of America was organized.

The original 1879 Ritty cash register

7

POLITICS

Ohio politicians have usually taken a middle-of-the-road course. They have rarely fought for laws exclusively to help the poor or the rich. It is probably because of the mixed population of the state—farmers, wealthy factory owners, and laborers.

Ohio is truly a middle-class society. As one writer said, "There is a dedication to the homely virtues of honesty, thrift, steadiness, caution, and a distrust of government." Ohio for the most part has had a balanced and stable economy, so its political leaders have not agitated for change. They have avoided extremes and maintained the good times.

Eight presidents, over a period of sixty years, have come from Ohio. They were William Henry Harrison, Ulysses S. Grant, Rutherford B. Hayes, James A. Garfield, Benjamin Harrison, William McKinley, William H. Taft, and Warren G. Harding.

All the Ohio presidents except Whig William Henry Harrison have been Republican. This does not mean that the state has given a rubber stamp to all its politicians. Norman Thomas, the Socialist presidential candidate for many years, was from Ohio, as was Virginia Claflin Woodhull, a flamboyant feminist who ran for the presidency in 1876.

—46

*Eight United States presidents
have come from Ohio, among
them William McKinley.*

Ohio's present state constitution, the second one it has had, was adopted in 1851. The governor is elected to a four-year term and is allowed to serve an unlimited number of terms as long as there are no more than two in succession.

The General Assembly consists of a thirty-three-member Senate and a ninety-nine-member House of Representatives. Senators serve four-year terms, representatives two-year terms. Regular legislative sessions begin on the first Monday of January in odd-numbered years and have no time limit.

An amendment to the Constitution may be proposed by either the state legislature, a petition signed by 10 percent of the voters, or a constitutional convention. A convention may be called if it is approved by two-thirds of each house and by a majority of the voters. Ohioans also vote every twenty years as to whether they wish to call a convention.

Ohio has eighty-eight counties. All the counties except one are governed by an elected three-member board of commissioners. Summit County is governed by an elected county executive and a seven-member council. The frontier democracy developed in the state's early history has survived.

KEEPING THE
WATER CLEAN

Concerned citizens are leading the way to preserve the natural resources of the state. Ohio has always been blessed with an abundance of water, but over the years increased population and industrial development have caused severe difficulties.

Lake Erie could not stand the onslaught. Commercial fishermen were the first to warn that the lake was dying. Algae was growing so thick that it was depleting water-borne oxygen for fish and blocking out sunlight needed for underwater plant life important for the marine food chain.

The Cuyahoga River that flows into Lake Erie at Cleveland had become a smelly dump site for raw sewage, oil, byproducts of steel making, chemical wastes, and trash, and actually caught fire on June 22, 1969. The event was given full television coverage, which instantly marred Cleveland's image as a garden city on the shore of sparkling Lake Erie.

One year later the U.S. Environmental Protection Agency was born. Cities and factories along the shoreline were forced to improve their waste disposal systems. Huge fines were levied on any municipality or industry that did not comply. Gradually, improvements

*Keeping Ohio's water clean has been
a leading priority of state officials.*

were seen. Lake Erie has been restocked with several varieties of fish, and now pleasure boats, as well as professional fishing boats, are coming up with prize catches.

The Ohio River was also going through a clean-up campaign. Nothing could change overnight, but when one of the sports writers for a national publication announced that good-tasting bass were now back in the Ohio, everyone knew that progress was being made.

The most difficult problem to control has been acid runoff from abandoned coal mines. The rocky strata around veins of coal contain several substances that, when exposed to the air and water, turn into iron sulfate and sulfuric acid. This cannot be stopped entirely, but the damage has been minimized in many cases by sealing off mines before the dangerous acid water can seep into underground water systems, contaminating wells and streams.

Ohio's canal traffic has ended, but the Ohio River is busier than ever. It carries more tonnage than the St. Lawrence Seaway and five times as much tonnage as the Panama Canal.

In the 1960s a new system of dams and locks was designed by the Corps of Engineers. Nineteen high-lift dams raise and lower the river a total of 427 feet (130.15 m). Each lock is 1,200 feet (305.41 m) long, large enough for the biggest tows. Channel depths are at a minimum of 12 feet (3.66 m), allowing a third more cargo in each barge and permitting the operation of bigger and more powerful diesel-powered towboats. These improvements lowered the cost of barge traffic by 50 percent, thus reducing the cost of electric power which relied on bulk quantities of coal, and in turn was a great benefit to hundreds of industrial plants.

The question arose whether there should be tolls on river traffic. It was pointed out that the original Ordinance of 1787 regarding the settlement of the Northwest Territory clearly stated that the navigable rivers leading into the Mississippi and the St. Lawrence should be common waterways and forever free.

Coal reserves of the valley are enormous. Low-cost coal is the key to the region's further industrial growth.

—51

River-front property is at a premium. New chemical plants are spreading on the upper river. Aluminum is the newest industry on the river, but iron and steel are still of utmost importance. As Andrew Carnegie once said, "Gold is precious, but iron is priceless."

Power stations with their multiple stacks as tall as sixty-story buildings are sharing space with plants using atomic energy. Engineers forever planning for the future are studying the cost and capacity of a rubber belt conveyor stretching from Lake Erie to the Ohio to carry coal, iron ore, and limestone to the mills on the river. Ohio has never been without its dreamers.

CITIES
AND PEOPLE

More than 60 percent of Ohio is still farmland, but three-quarters of her citizens live in city areas.

Ohio's cities are as varied as its crops. Geography, population, and industry cause the differences. Cleveland is the largest city in Ohio. In the early years, Cleveland was a small inland port settled by New Englanders. There were a few German merchants and some Irish dockworkers, but Cleveland still resembled a New England town.

In the years following the Civil War, surging commercial growth and industrialization brought to the city an influx of immigrants from eastern and southern Europe. By 1910 these immigrants made up 75 percent of the central city's population. Following World War II, there was a large number of new blacks from the South who helped make up the work force. There were times of racial unrest, particularly riots in 1968, but Cleveland can claim to have elected the first black mayor of a major American city, Carl B. Stokes.

Strong leadership has always been a factor in Cleveland's growth. Jephtha Wade, whose telegraph company evolved into the Western Union Company, John D. Rockefeller, founder of the Standard Oil

Above: *the skyline of Cleveland*
Right: *an oil refinery in Cleveland*

Company, and Charles F. Brush, who invented the carbon arc lamp that used to light the city's streets, are just a few who were influential in the city's early development.

Cincinnati once could claim to be the largest and most cosmopolitan city of the new West. It sprang to prominence because of its docks on the Ohio River. Although it has always had a number of large manufacturing businesses, it has been considered a commercial center and a market exchange. Before the Civil War, its main trade was with southern states. There planters raised crops of cotton and corn and sold or traded them for flour, salt pork, whiskey, and household items not produced on plantations.

Cincinnati was originally settled by Germans, and even today, near the Fountain Center and Government Squares, there are smoke-stained buildings built by German craftsmen a hundred and fifty years ago. Cincinnati had a grand hotel, an elegant opera house, and gambling houses equal to almost anything found east of the Appalachians.

When the railroads took over much of the traffic from the river boats, Cincinnati suffered a slump in prosperity. It also suffered from the hold of a political machine headed by boss George Barnsdale Cox. Corruption followed. At one time, Cincinnati was known for having the worst city government in the country. After twenty-five years of rule, a set of reform candidates were finally elected in 1922. They cleaned up both local politics and the city, putting Cincinnati back on the map again as a leader in business and cultural affairs.

The smoky haze that once hung over the city has almost entirely disappeared with modern-day regulations for pollution control. The city turns out tools, bakery goods, textbooks, medicines, shoes, soap, radios, processed foods, and playing cards. It is still a vast marketplace.

Columbus, the capital of Ohio, is situated in almost the exact geographical center of the state. It spreads out over the rolling Scioto Valley. It has always been at the crossroads of traffic, whether

Indian trails, Zane's Trace, the first overland turnpike in the West, canal traffic, or today with rail, highway, and air connections.

Some say that Columbus is made up of three cities. One is centered around the gray stone capitol in its ten-acre square. Another is the sprawling campus of Ohio State University, one of the largest and best-known academic centers in the country. The third area of Columbus includes the various commercial and industrial complexes that are spreading from the center of town in every direction. Many kinds of heavy equipment are manufactured there—fire trucks, concrete-mixing machinery, and mining machinery.

Large glass skyscrapers spike the middle of the city near the river, but the citizens of Columbus have also taken care to preserve some of the beautiful older brick buildings in "German Village." There is also an Italian section, but over the years the city has assimilated its many ethnic groups.

A large military base has always been situated in Columbus, and the city is known as a principal banking center.

Akron, once known as a busy port at the intersection of two canal routes, has since gained fame by being the rubber capital of the world. The canals brought a rowdy and, so the story goes, somewhat scandalous element to the city, but all were welcomed at the gristmills and the pottery works before the coming of Goodrich and Firestone.

The old canals have been filled in. Great viaducts cut across the river valley, and huge factories can be seen in every direction. Everything from rubber washers to space suits for astronauts are made in Akron. Automobile tires by the millions and lighter-than-air craft are manufactured there.

Cincinnati's early prominence in the state was due partly to its many docks on the Ohio River.

The models of woolly mammoths at the Cincinnati Museum of Natural History. The exhibit depicts a Cincinnati landscape as museum scientists believe it appeared about 10,000 years ago.

Because so much of the labor force was involved with the rubber industry, the well-being of the town followed the same pattern as the factories. Today there is much more diversification, and the economy is healthier. From the standpoint of research, Akron is perhaps the nation's fastest-growing city. Both Firestone and Goodrich have laboratories there, where scientists are searching for new ways to put plastics and rubber to use.

Toledo stretches for fifteen miles along both sides of the Maumee River, a short distance from Maumee Bay at the westernmost tip of Lake Erie. It is the third largest port on the Great Lakes, outranked only by Duluth and Buffalo. It is the world's greatest shipper of bituminous coal.

Many ethnic groups are represented in Toledo. The Germans came first. Then Polish, Hungarian, English, and Irish people arrived. Many individuals came from Canada, too.

When an abundant supply of natural gas was discovered in the Maumee Valley, new industries flocked to Toledo, principally glass works. The Libbey Glass Company was founded, manufacturing high-grade crystal and lamp globes. Later, rolling mills were developed to produce plate glass. Glass building blocks were another product.

At the turn of the century, Toledo was the nation's third largest railroad center. In 1908 John Willy came to town and started to build automobiles. Other related products manufactured there were Champion spark plugs and automobile gears.

The money that swamped the town overflowed into cultural improvements such as a fine university and an art museum.

For twenty-five miles along the Mahoning River Valley in eastern Ohio, smokestacks from steel mills dominate the scenery. Youngstown is at the center of the activity. It is a mill town closely tied to the steel industry. Since its first crude smelter was started in 1802, Youngstown has been considered a mill city. It was close to the raw products used in the industry—coal, ore, and limestone.

It became the fourth largest producer of pig iron and steel in

The Firestone Tire and Rubber Company's world headquarters in Akron

Glass tumblers being stamped on the bottom with identification numbers at the Libbey Glass Company in Toledo

the United States. The town's favorable location for manufacturing, warehousing, and distribution has helped diversify the industry in the last decade, as the steel industry has declined. There are many large companies involved with making equipment for the mills and with processing its products into finished items.

Dayton spreads over a great flood plain and into the surrounding hills of the Miami Valley, fifty miles north of Cincinnati at the forks of the Great Miami River. Four streams unite in the heart of modern Dayton.

Because of the geography of the area, Dayton suffered severe flooding several times. In 1918 a four-year plan to control the waters of the Miami Valley was started. Dikes and channel improvements were constructed which have held the water back even during the heaviest run-off.

Scattered through the city are factories, mostly of the light-industry, precision type. It is the home of the National Cash Register Company and Frigidaire, both well-known trademarks of American business.

Dayton is a city of little smoke and congestion. It is proud of its many parks and of its history of being the home of the Wright brothers. It was in Dayton that the world's first wind tunnel was built to prove the use of the rudderlike ailerons in controlling flight of a heavier-than-air craft. For a brief time, Dayton was the hub of aircraft manufacture. The old-time De Haviland planes used in France during World War I came from Dayton.

Each time America mobilized for war—from the Civil War to present worldwide conflicts—Ohio factories have been major suppliers of goods. Between profit-making expansions, there have been recessions in heavy industry. So it has been for the last decade, with Ohio suffering an economic loss.

There has been competition from overseas, from Europe and from the Far East. Foreign cars and importation of steel have broken the long-standing monopoly Ohio's factories and mills had in the world market.

Youngstown, Ohio, was hard hit by this new competition. It was a mill town where almost the entire labor force was engaged in the job of turning out steel. The mills were antiquated and inefficient. Wages were much higher in the United States than in foreign countries.

Gradually, the larger mills closed their doors, and unemployment rose alarmingly. The once prosperous area was soon dubbed the "rust bowl."

A few enterprising mill owners faced the problem and decided to do something about it. By cutting the size of their operations, updating equipment, and specializing in certain products where there was less competition, they've been able to make a profit. Using scrap iron, which this country stockpiles in quantity, has added more savings.

One reason for Ohio's temporary lag in the economy is the significant shift in dollar income to the sun-belt states of the South and Southwest. This came about primarily through the technical developments in computer-related industries. There was no reason for these highly specialized plants to be built in the shadows of the outmoded heavy-industry factories in the Midwest. They did not have to be situated close to the source of material supply. Fine climate and good working conditions lured the new work force away from Ohio.

Leaders in the state did not sit back idly and let the industrial and business community of Ohio die. New products and new markets for old products were the answer. Fretting about the compe-

Above: *downtown Youngstown, a city hard hit by foreign competition and suffering from an economic decline.* Below: *one of Youngstown's only existing steel mills.*

*Ohio Governor Richard F. Celeste (right) at
ribbon-cutting ceremonies for the opening of
J. C. Penney Insurance Company headquarters
in Columbus. State leaders are actively seeking
new industries and new products for the state.*
Top: *a fish-eye aerial view of Columbus*
Bottom: *Ohio is a state filled with scenic beauty.*

tition of imports led the planners to consider how they could turn the tide of trade. How could they stimulate Ohio's production for export to foreign countries? State agencies were set up to help companies of all sizes market their wares abroad.

The most recent Census Bureau figures estimate that materials and parts incorporated in exported products accounted for 14.8 percent of Ohio's manufacturing output. Machinery, transportation equipment, chemicals, and farm products headed the list. The "rust bowl" is now gleaming with new structures built with new capital.

Weather, topography, location, soil, and mineral wealth all had a part in making Ohio great, but one of the prime factors in creating this state of superlatives was the people who lived there—the pioneer settlers, political leaders, scientists, industrialists, and those who labored to put dreams into practical focus.

Ohio is still growing, still changing, still producing individuals to lead us into the future. What better examples do we have than John Glenn, the first American astronaut to orbit the earth, and Neil Armstrong, the first person to set foot on the moon? Both are from Ohio, as was Judith Resnik, the second woman astronaut from this country, who lost her life on the Challenger mission.

Ohio has always supplied men and women in all fields of leadership. No doubt it will continue to do so.

Astronaut Judith Resnick, killed in the Challenger *disaster, was an Ohioan.*

FOR FURTHER
READING

Carter, William. *Middle West Country*. Boston: Houghton Mifflin, 1975.

Havighurst, Walter. *Ohio, a Bicentennial History*. New York: Norton, 1976.

———. *River to the West*. New York: Putnam, 1970.

Pierce, Neal R., and John Keefe. *The Great Lakes of America.* New York: Norton, 1980.

Smith, Thomas H., ed. *An Ohio Reader*. Grand Rapids, Mich.: Eerdmans, 1975.

INDEX

Akron, 27, 29, 42–43, 57, 59, 60
Aluminum refining, 43
American Federation of Labor, 45
Anchor Fire Hose Company, 42
Antitrust laws, 43, 45
Armstrong, Neil, 67
Army of the Shenandoah, 38

Battle of Fallen Timbers, 18
Battle of the Thames, 23
Blacks, 53
Burnet House, 31

Canal Project, the, 26–27
Canal traffic, 51
Canoe passages, 26
Chance, Alec, 40
Chase, Salmon P., 38

Cincinnati, 20, 26, 31–32, 39, 55, 56
Civil War, 35–38
Cleveland, 11, 25, 40, 42, 53–55
Coal industry, 42, 45, 51
Coffin, Levi, and "Aunt Katie," 36
Columbus, 23, 32, 36, 55, 57, 65
Computer-related industries, 62
Conestoga wagons, 25
Cox, George Barnsdale, 55
Cultural life, 32–35
Cuyahoga River, 17, 49

Dams and lock systems, 51
Dayton, 61

Eagle Iron Works, 39
Edison, Thomas Alva, 43
Education, 33

English traders, 17, 18
Erie Canal, 26

Farming, 11, 14, 20, 23, 27
Farm machinery, 39
Firestone, 42−43, 57, 59, 60
First settlers, 15, 17−18, 20, 27,
    38, 53, 57
Flagler, Henry, 40
Floating barnyards, 25−26
French and Indian War, 18
French traders, 15, 17−18

Garfield, James A., 38, 46
Gas refineries, 40, 42
Geddess, James, 26
Glass and clay products, 42
Glenn, John, 67
Gompers, Samuel, 45
Goodrich, 42, 57, 59
Goodyear, Charles, 43
Grain, 29
Grant, Ulysses S., 37, 38, 46

Harding, Warren G., 46
Harrison, Benjamin, 46
Harrison, William, 23, 46
Hayes, Rutherford B., 38, 46

Immigrants, 20, 27, 38, 53, 57
Indians, 15, 17−18, 23
Industry and labor, 14, 39−45
    competition in, 61−62, 67
International Business Ma-
    chines Corporation, 43

Inventors, 42
Iron and steel industry, 59, 61

Labor unions, 45
Lake Erie, 7, 11, 17, 23, 25−26,
    39, 42, 49, 51
"Lake Ohio," 9
Land law of 1787, 20
Land Ordinance of 1785, 18
Libbey Glass Company, 59, 60
Lincoln, Abraham, 35, 38

McGuffey's readers. *See New
    England Primer*
McKinley, William, 46, 47
Mad River and Lake Erie line, 31
Miami-Erie Canal, 26−27
Miami University, 33
Morrow, Jeremiah, 26

National Cash Register Corpo-
    ration, 43, 61
National Road, 25, 36
Natural resources, 9, 49−52
New England Primer, 33, 35
Northwest Territory, 18, 23, 33,
    51

Oberlin College, 33
Ohio
    area, 7, 9, 14
    cities, 53−67
    climate, 9, 11, 14
    commercial development, 39
    crops, 14, 27, 29

Ohio (*continued*)
    economy, 61–62, 67
    history, 9, 15–23
    mineral resources, 9, 11
    population, 14, 24
    products, 27
    rainfall, 11
    state government, 23, 48
    waterways, 26, 49–52
Ohio Canal, 26–27
Ohio Federation of Labor, 45
Ohio Oil, 45
Ohio River, 7, 15, 17, 25–26, 39, 51
Ohio University, 33, 57
Ohio Valley, 9, 15, 17–18, 20
Oil refineries, 40, 41, 54

Perry, Oliver Hazard, 22, 23
Pollution control, 55

Quakers, 36

Railroads, 29–31, 42
Republicans, 46
Resnik, Judith, 66, 67
Ritty, John, 43, 44
Rockefeller, John D., 40, 45, 53, 55
Rubber industry, 42, 57, 59

Sheridan, Philip H., 38
Sherman, John, 43, 45
Sherman, William T., 38
Slavery, 33–35

Soil conservation, 11, 13, 14
Stagecoach travel, 25
Standard Oil Company, 40, 45, 53, 55
Stanton, Edwin M., 38
Steamboats, 26
Stokes, Carl B., 53
Stowe, Harriet Beecher, 34, 35

Taft, William H., 46
Tecumseh, 23
Territorial Congress, 18
Thomas, Norman, 46
Toledo, 7, 25, 29, 31, 59
Transportation, 24–31, 36

Uncle Tom's Cabin, 35
Underground railroad, 36
United Mine Workers, 45
U.S. Environmental Protection Agency, 49, 51

Wade, Jephta, 53
War of 1812, 22, 23
War of Independence, 18
Western Reserve, 18, 20
Western Union Company, 53
Willy, John, 59
Woodhull, Virginia Claflin, 46
Wright, Orville and Wilbur, 43, 61

Youngstown, 59, 61–62, 63

Zane's Trace, 24–25, 57
Zoarites, 27

ABOUT THE AUTHOR

Mary Virginia Fox, known to her friends as Ginger, was born in Richmond, Virginia, but has lived most of her life in the Midwest. She attended Northwestern University where she earned an honors degree in the field of art.

Her first short story was published in a magazine when she was only twelve, and she has been writing ever since. She has written twenty-five books for young adults and many shorter pieces of fiction and nonfiction in collections, as well as feature and travel articles for adult readers.

Ms. Fox and her husband have lived overseas in the Philippines, Iran, Colombia, and Tunisia. Traveling is a second hobby in addition to her art work. She and her husband live on the shores of Lake Mendota across the water from Madison, Wisconsin.